WOLFPACK

ALSO BY ABBY WAMBACH

Wolfpack: How to Come Together,
Unleash Our Power, and Change the Game

Forward: A Memoir

WOLFPACK

How Young People Will
Find Their Voice, Unite Their Pack,
and Change the World

ABBY WAMBACH

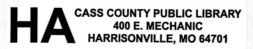

Roaring Brook Press
New York

Published by Roaring Brook Press
Roaring Brook Press is a division of Holtzbrinck Publishing
Holdings Limited Partnership
120 Broadway, New York, NY 10271
mackids.com

Library of Congress Control Number: 2020940006
ISBN 978-1-250-76686-1

Our books may be purchased in bulk for promotional,
educational, or business use. Please contact your local
bookseller or the Macmillan Corporate and Premium Sales
Department at (800) 221-7945 ext. 5442 or by email at
MacmillanSpecialMarkets@macmillan.com.

First edition, 2020
Book design by Aurora Parlagreco
Printed in the United States of America by LSC
Communications, Harrisonburg, Virginia

3 5 7 9 10 8 6 4 2

To our youngest daughter, Amma,
Whose howl makes me Brave.
And for all the young people:
May you change the world,
Always knowing the Power of your Wolf
And the Love of your Pack.

CONTENTS

WELCOME TO THE WOLFPACK

Imagine that you've been asked to give a graduation speech at one of the premier colleges in the nation. You've got fifteen minutes to stand behind a podium in a fancy robe and tell hundreds of brilliant young people everything you know about:

> What makes a good life,
> What makes a beautiful world, and
> How to build both.

Would it make you stop and think hard about what you believe?

Would it make you feel overwhelmed and underqualified?

Might it even lead you to sweat all over and wonder

if a person who hasn't even graduated from college should really give a graduation speech?

(Maybe that last worry was uniquely mine.)

A few years ago, I was asked to deliver such a speech at Radio City Music Hall in New York City to the 126th graduating class of Barnard College, a women's liberal arts college in Manhattan.

The invitation said:

> We are awed by your talents on the field, but we are also moved by your commitment to issues like gender equality, pay inequity, and gay rights. Our seniors would be thrilled to have you address them at this watershed moment in their lives.

I sat on my couch, read those words twice, and then grabbed my phone and googled: *watershed moment.* (FYI: It means "turning point" or "historic moment.")

Then I thought:

Okay.

They don't want me to speak as just an athlete. They want me to speak as an activist and leader.

At one of the most important moments in their lives.

No pressure.

The invitation went on to say:

> Former Barnard speakers have included: Barack Obama, Hillary Clinton, and Meryl Streep.

No big deal, I thought. *Only a former U.S. president, the first woman in American history to win the popular vote for the presidency, and the most accomplished actor of all time.*

More sweat.

For the last few years, I had been traveling and speaking to people all over the world as a famous athlete. I spoke about my personal life, my time on the field, and how to win championships.

I was a decorated soccer champion.

I'd scored more international goals than any woman or man in history.

I'd won two Olympic gold medals and a FIFA World Cup championship.

That stuff was cool. But since I was a kid, what I loved most about soccer was being a teammate and a leader.

I loved winning and losing as ONE team.

I loved being a part of something bigger than myself.

I loved the shared joy, suffering, failure, and success.

I loved the magic of collectively surrendering to an unknown outcome.

I loved the closeness of our team dinners, bus rides, and stinky locker rooms.

I loved how my teammates and I cared for each other, fought for each other, and respected each other—no matter what.

What I loved most about soccer was being a teammate to women and a leader of women.

As co-captain of the United States women's national soccer team, I was charged with uniting twenty-three women—each of whom had achieved success because of her individual talent—and inspiring each to commit to the group, the collective. With the help of my teammates, I created a team culture based on more than just excellence. We not only won, we won with joy, honor, connectedness, commitment, and sisterhood. We were not only champions on the field—we were champions of each other. Our time on the U.S. Women's National Team turned us into more than just winners. We turned each other into better friends, citizens, and human beings.

When I retired, I missed my team and the unique connection that is forged among a group of people working toward a common goal. But as I sat and looked at that invitation, I had this thought:

What if my time on the national team was just practice for a bigger game?

What if I could find a way to translate our team's culture to more people?

What if I could inspire a broader team off the field, too?

The Barnard women would enter Radio City Music Hall as college students and leave as adults. What if I entered as Abby, a leader on the soccer field, and left as Abby, a leader in the world?

I was scared—but I said yes to Barnard anyway. I said yes for those women, but also for myself. The Barnard women weren't the only ones stepping off into an unknown future, reinventing themselves, trying to find their way in the world. I was right there with them. This speech would be a watershed moment for me, too.

First, though, I had to actually write the darned thing.

There was a moment in every soccer game when I'd feel the energy shift toward me. Whether it was a morale boost, a momentum swing, or a goal that we needed—it was my job to make it happen. When I felt that shift, I'd say silently to myself:

Let's go, Abby. It's your time.

As I sat down to prepare my speech, that's what I told myself. I needed this rally cry, too. Giving a speech to young people at this moment in our world's history felt sacred and daunting. We were at a crossroads.

There were so many confusing messages to sort through. On the one hand, humanity had made enormous progress on big problems. More children were being educated, fewer people were living in extreme poverty, and it seemed—for a while—that growing numbers of people were becoming less tolerant of bigotry. At the same time, grave dangers were on the rise from climate change; rampant racial, religious, and gender discrimination; and a deepening divisiveness among Americans. It felt like a real possibility that the clock would be turned back on so much of the progress we'd made over the last century for equality.

I wanted to believe that I could make a difference. I wanted to believe that I could help these graduates believe that *they* could make a difference. Because I knew then, as I know now, that young people are this world's great hope. But I also knew that this would be a heavy message for those kids to hear. They would know how much I was asking of them. Saving the world is a big challenge to accept. It might have seemed impossible, even.

But I don't believe in impossible. Because the lesson of my life has been: a group of passionate people who unite for a larger goal can achieve the impossible again and again.

As I focused on what I wanted to share with the women of Barnard—a directive to unleash their individuality, unite the collective, and change the world—my thoughts turned to a TED Talk video I'd watched recently about the wolves of Yellowstone National Park.

In 1995, wolves were reintroduced into Yellowstone after being absent for seventy years. It was a controversial decision, but rangers decided it was a risk worth taking, because the land was in trouble. During those seventy years, the number of deer skyrocketed because they were alone and unchallenged at the top of the food chain. They grazed unchecked and reduced the plant life so severely that the riverbanks eroded.

Once a small number of wolves arrived, big changes started happening almost immediately.

First, they thinned out the deer through hunting. But more important, the presence of the wolves drastically changed the behavior of the remaining deer. Wisely, the deer started avoiding the places they'd be most vulnerable to the wolves—the valleys—and the vegetation in those places grew back. The trees grew five times higher in just six years. Birds and beavers started moving in. The beavers built river dams, which provided habitats for otters and ducks and fish. Ravens and bald eagles returned to eat the carrion: meat and bones left over by the wolves. Bears came back because berries started growing again.

But that wasn't all. The rivers actually changed as well. The plant regrowth stabilized the riverbanks, so they stopped collapsing. The rivers flowed freely again.

In short:

> The plant ecosystem grew back.
> The animal ecosystem grew back.
> The entire landscape changed.
> All because of the wolves' presence.

See what happened there?

The wolves—who were feared by many to be a threat to the system—became the system's *salvation*.

Now, look around our world today: *See what's happening here?*

Young people—maybe you, like the wolves of Yellowstone—are dismissed and underestimated. Maybe you, like the wolves, will become the world's salvation.

You are the ones we've been waiting for.

YOU.
ARE.
THE.
WOLVES.

Your Wolfpack is your entire generation. Throughout my life, my Wolfpack was my soccer team. So I know that every Wolfpack needs a unifying structure. The most effective way to create a collective heartbeat is to establish rules for the Pack to live by.

The U.S. Women's National Team is a unique thing: an all-women ecosystem separated, in many ways, from the larger system. FIFA (the international governing body of the sport) largely ignores and devalues women's soccer. The women are on their own. They know if they want respect and a future for the sport, they have to create it themselves. They are a pack of wolves set on changing the landscape of our sport.

In 1999, two years before I joined them, the national team went to FIFA and said, "We're going to play in professional football stadiums for the World Cup like the men do."

FIFA said, "No. Women don't play in those venues.

You'll never sell enough tickets." In other words: *Stay in your place. Follow the old rules. Don't be ridiculous.* (Note: When they say you're ridiculous, you know you're onto something.)

The U.S. Women's National Team ignored those warnings and set out to build what they dreamed of. How? By reaching out to the young girls and boys who loved soccer as much as they did. They visited schools and spoke to gymnasiums full of kids. They surprised teams of young girls on soccer pitches. They once drove by a youth soccer tournament and asked the bus driver to pull over so they could talk to the kids about the World Cup. They were scrappy and they sacrificed. They were zero ego and all heart. They were united and committed to a vision that they knew was possible and were determined to bring to life. This was a grassroots campaign—if they couldn't get backing from the FIFA executives at the top, they'd grow their support from the ground up. It was how they planned to rise high enough to shatter the glass ceiling, that invisible barrier that keeps women out of positions of power.

And they did. They sold out stadiums. They created the most powerful women's sports movement the world had ever seen, and the biggest event in the history of women's sports. Their final game, played at the Rose Bowl in Pasadena in 1999, was attended by more than 90,000 people—the largest crowd to ever attend a women's sporting event in history. It was also the most-watched soccer game in the U.S. to date, including any men's World Cup matches. With 40 million people around the world watching the game live, it garnered higher ratings than the finals for both professional hockey and basketball. There were suddenly new rules to the game—written by those women—but only because a bunch of unstoppable visionaries had the courage to break the old ones.

As Ava DuVernay, the first black woman to direct a film nominated for an Academy Award for Best Picture, said:

> *Regarding glass ceilings . . . I'm mostly bolstered by folks who create their own ceilings. I'm less interested in banging down the door of some man who doesn't want me there. I'm more about building my own house.*

The message I decided to share with the Barnard students—the message of this book—is this: Young people must stop following the Old Rules, which exist only to maintain the status quo, the way things are right now. Old ways of thinking will never help us build a new world. Out with the Old, in with the New.

Welcome to the Wolfpack Way—8 New Rules to Help Young People Change the World.

ONE

YOU WERE ALWAYS THE WOLF

Old Rule: Stay on the path.
New Rule: Create your own path.

Like most children who grew up when I did, I was taught to keep my head down, stay on the path, and get my job done. I was freaking Little Red Riding Hood.

You know the fairy tale—it's just one version of the stories kids are told the world over. Little Red Riding Hood heads off through the woods having been given strict instructions: Stay on the path. Don't talk to anybody. Keep your head down and hidden beneath your protective red cape.

And she follows the rules . . . at first. But then she dares to get a little curious and she ventures off the path. That's, of course, when she encounters the Big Bad Wolf and the tale takes a sharp turn for the worse.

The message of these stories is clear:

Follow the rules.

Don't be curious.

Don't say too much.

Don't expect more.

Otherwise, bad things will happen.

But when I look out into the world, as well as back on my life, it becomes clear to me that those stories aren't true. Every good thing that has come to me—and to the people I respect—has happened when we dared to venture off the path.

When I was young, I was told: "Good girls wear dresses."

I hated wearing dresses.

I'd look at myself in the mirror when I was wearing a dress and the pit in my stomach would rise to my throat. I'd stare at myself and think: *I don't like how this looks or how this feels. This is not me.*

I felt the need to hold my breath from the second that dress went on until the second I pulled it off. It felt like I was in costume, hiding who I really was in order to fit in, to be good.

The question of my childhood was: *Why can't I wear what I want to wear?*

When I got to my all-girls high school, the rules seemed to change.

I remember sitting in classrooms witnessing the complete character shifts of some of my friends. Girls who were quiet with our guy friends became chatty and opinionated in our all-girls environment. Girls who rarely ate a thing around the boys started chowing down during our lunch periods. And it wasn't just the way we acted and ate that changed without boys around. How we dressed changed, too. At our school, we dressed for comfort, not attention. I learned that people do not have to dress to impress. We can dress for ourselves. We can wear on the outside how we feel on the inside. We can choose our own comfort even if it makes other people uncomfortable.

I dated boys in high school, because my religious upbringing and culture taught me that this was what girls were supposed to do. Boys were fine, I guess. It wasn't until I felt that spark of deep affection with a girl that I realized love is supposed to be more than just fine. Out of fear of losing my family, I decided that being openly gay wasn't an option for me. I was sure they wouldn't approve. This broke my heart.

The question of my teenage years was: *Why can't I love who I want to love?*

I tried to keep this part of myself buried for as long as I could. Then, during my senior year in high school, I experienced real love for the first time. This love felt as important and necessary as air, as food, as shelter. I began my first gay relationship like many gay people did back then—in secret. The secrecy felt equal parts enraging and exciting. I couldn't tell anyone, so I felt afraid and isolated from my family and friends. But I also learned that real love is a human need and that if I denied myself of it, some part of me would die. Trembling—and secretly for a long while—I chose love. I chose myself.

Later, I began to dream of becoming a professional soccer player. The problem was that women's professional soccer was so new and overlooked that I didn't even know it existed. So I'd watch the U.S. Men's

National Team play and think: *But I could do that. I want to do that.*

The question of my twenties was: *Why can't I become what I want to become?*

Little did I know that behind the scenes, women were creating the opportunities that I would one day seize and build my career upon. Women were fighting for Title IX—a law that bars discrimination against women so that schools must spend as much money on women's sports as they do on men's sports. Women were building professional women's leagues, and demanding a livable wage for the emerging women's national soccer team. They even went on strike—refusing to work until they got paid better. By the time I left college, women I'd never met had begun to clear the path I would walk. The way forward was suddenly wider. It held more options for me and fewer dangers.

Those women did not hide under a cape and keep to the trail. In fact, there had been no path for them, so they made a new one. They laid that new path—brick by brick—for generations of women to follow. They created things for me that I didn't even know I needed. They spent their lives and careers building something that many of them knew they'd never get to take advantage of—but they did it anyway.

For a long time, I had stayed on the path out of fear, not of being eaten by a wolf, but of not being accepted or loved; of getting cut from the team or benched; of not being able to play the game at the highest level.

Little by little, I started to recognize the collective effort of all of the leaders that came before me. And, little by little, I discovered a truth about myself. If I could go back and tell my younger self one thing, it would be this:

Abby,
You were never Little Red Riding Hood.
You were always the Wolf.

There is a wolf inside of you. Your wolf is who you were made to be before the world told you who to be. Your wolf is your talent, your power, your dreams, your voice, your curiosity, your courage, your dignity, your choices—your truest identity.

CALL TO THE WOLFPACK:

Wear what you want. Love who you love.
Become what you imagine.
Create what you need.
You were never Little Red Riding Hood.
You were always the Wolf.

TWO

BE GRATEFUL *AND* AMBITIOUS

Old Rule: Be grateful for what you have.

New Rule: Be grateful for what you have AND demand what you deserve.

At the end of my soccer career, ESPN decided to honor me with their Icon Award. I'd accept the award at the ESPYS—their nationally televised show—along with two other retiring champions: the basketball star Kobe Bryant and the football quarterback Peyton Manning.

I was excited. This felt like a big deal. My first thought was: *What am I going to wear?*

My answer was: exactly what I want to wear, sneakers and all. I got my new suit tailored. I bought some sparkly sneakers. I got my head freshly bleached and shaved. Why not go for soccer icon and fashion icon on the same night?

The night of the ESPYS the musician Justin Timberlake, the presenter of our awards, stood on stage and showed highlight videos of our careers to the audience. He talked about what we three had in common: our talent, our grit, our dedication. As he described the lengths we were willing to go, he showed footage of me getting my bloody head stapled back together during a game. He stopped and said, with shock and awe: "They stapled. Her head."

The crowd squirmed and laughed, which made me feel super tough—worthy of the stage I was standing on.

When it was time for us to receive our awards, the three of us stood together while the cameras rolled and the audience cheered. I don't know how Kobe and Peyton felt in that moment, but I felt overwhelming gratitude. I was so grateful to be there—to be included in the company of Kobe and Peyton. I had a momentary feeling of having arrived, like women athletes had finally made it.

Then the applause ended, and it was time for the three of us to exit stage left. As I watched those men walk off the stage, it dawned on me that while the three of us were stepping away from similar careers, we were facing very different futures.

Each of us—Kobe, Peyton, and I—had made the

same sacrifices for our careers; shed the same amount of blood, sweat, and tears; won world championships at the same level. We'd left it all on the field for decades with the same ferocity, talent, and commitment. But our retirements wouldn't be the same at all. Because Kobe and Peyton were walking off that stage and into their futures with something I didn't have: Enormous bank accounts. Because of that they had something else I didn't have: Freedom. Their hustling days were over. Mine were just beginning.

After the ESPYS that night, back in my hotel room, I lay in bed and finally acknowledged what had been simmering inside me for decades: Anger.

In the 2018 FIFA Men's World Cup the winning team took home $38 million in prize money—that's nineteen times the amount that the winning team brought home in the 2015 FIFA Women's World Cup. Nineteen times more. This despite the fact that in 2015, when the U.S. Women's National Team won the World Cup championship, the Women's National Team turned a profit of $6.6 million, whereas the Men's National Team earned a profit of just under $2 million.

How did FIFA explain away this injustice? They

liked to claim that the men had more fans, without acknowledging that they themselves built that lopsided fanbase by marketing, championing, and funding only the men's teams for over a century. Investing money and resources into salaries, advertising, merchandise, and television broadcasting gets more people to pay attention and become loyal fans—creating the differences in fanbase size between men's sports and women's sports. The imbalance that the system points to as the excuse for inequity is actually *created* by the system itself! Why didn't FIFA begin investing in the women just like they'd invested in the men for so long?

I was angry at myself for not speaking up more about this glaring discrimination and obvious injustice during my soccer career. I was angry for my teammates, for my mentors, for all women. Because I knew that this wasn't just about me, and it wasn't just about sports.

My story is every woman's story.

On average, women across the globe will earn significantly less than men in the same types of jobs throughout their careers, a pay gap that widens over time. In the beginning of 2018, women in the U.S.

earned 81.1 percent of what their male counterparts earned across all industries and ages—which is about 81 cents for every dollar earned by a man. Studies have shown that, on average, women must work sixty-six extra days in order to earn the same salary as their male counterparts. Wage inequity is even more devastating for women of color: Black women are typically paid only 63 cents, and Latinas only 54 cents, for every dollar paid to their white, male counterparts.

Think of it this way: Imagine that a girl in your class walks your neighbor's dog and gets paid six bucks each time. After a few weeks, she'd have a nice bit of cash. Maybe she'd feel grateful at first. But how would you feel if you found out your neighbor paid a boy in your class ten dollars each time he walked that dog? How would you feel knowing that a girl got paid less for doing the same exact job a boy did? Would you feel shocked? Angry? Would you speak up and ask some hard questions? Hopefully you would.

I spent most of my time during my career the same way I'd spent my time on that ESPYS stage. Just feeling grateful. I was so grateful for a paycheck, so grateful to represent my country, so grateful to be the token woman—one of the few women, or sometimes the only woman—getting recognition, so grateful to receive any respect at all that I was afraid to use my voice to demand more for myself—and equality for all of us.

Our gratitude for what we have should never keep us from speaking out. It is okay to demand equality. It is okay to demand more. It is okay to be a little bit angry about unfairness in the world, and to use that anger to help level the playing field for all of us.

CALL TO THE WOLFPACK:

Be grateful.
But do not JUST be grateful.
Be grateful AND brave.
Be grateful AND ambitious.
Be grateful AND righteous.
Be grateful AND persistent.
Be grateful AND loud.
Be grateful for what you have AND demand
what you deserve.

THREE

LEAD FROM THE BENCH

Old Rule: Wait for permission to lead.

New Rule: Lead now—from wherever you are.

When you think of leaders, who do you imagine? Presidents? Teachers? Coaches?

I know that's who I usually think of. Here's my question: Why don't you think of yourself?

Maybe because our understanding of leadership has left out too many of us for too long. Especially young people. Sometimes being a kid can feel like you're constantly being benched. Like you're waiting to grow up so you can get in the game. But I believe that leaders lead from wherever they are—no matter what.

2015 was a big year for me. As co-captain of the U.S. Women's National Team I was helping to lead us to a World Cup championship. Part of my job was to work with the coaching staff to assemble the eleven starters who would give us the best chance to win the tournament.

We had some hard decisions to make.

After the first few games, it became clear that I didn't belong on that starting roster anymore. At thirty-five, I was one of the oldest players on the team. I had lost a step and I was suffering from nagging and constant pain in different parts of my body, from years of playing hard and getting injured. I wasn't the player I used to be. The team knew it, the coaches knew it, I knew it.

So imagine this: You've scored more international goals in your sport than any human being on the planet. You've co-captained and led Team USA to victory after victory for the past decade. And you and your coach sit down and decide together that you won't be a starter for the remainder of your final World Cup. Instead, you'll be a substitute. You'll come off the bench.

This was hard to accept as Abby Wambach, co-captain of Team USA. It was even harder to accept as Abby, the competitive kid who dreamed of leading her team to victory on the field as I had so many times before.

But if I had not been stuck on that bench for the World Cup, I would not have learned the most important lesson of leadership, the one I want all young people everywhere to understand. I knew how to lead on the field. Now I needed to learn how to lead from the bench.

The second game of the tournament arrived. I was accustomed to walking out onto the field in front of the roaring crowd while holding the hand of a wide-eyed kid, in line with the other starters. We'd walk to the center of the field, face the flags, and listen to our country's anthem. This was my pregame ritual and one of the honors of my career. But this time I walked into the stadium with the reserve players, stopped in front of our bench—and watched another set of eleven players put their hands over their hearts for the anthem.

I knew that the eyes of the crowd, my teammates, and my fans were on me. They were all watching to see how I would react. I had a choice between pouting and making this moment about me or swallowing my pride and making it about our team.

When I was on the field, what inspired and motivated me most was not the millions of strangers cheering, but when my teammates paid attention, saw me, and believed in me. I thought of my long-time teammate and friend Lori Lindsey. We'd played together since we were fifteen years old. Lori wasn't a consistent starter on the national team, but she made our team better because she put as much energy into cheering from the bench as some players did when they played ninety minutes. So I channeled Lori.

I paid attention. I screamed so loudly, obnoxiously, and relentlessly that the coach moved me to the far side of the bench. I kept water ready for players coming off the field. I celebrated when goals were scored, and I kept believing in us even when mistakes were made. I knew the women on the field like sisters, so I could predict, in every moment, exactly what each needed from me. Whatever it was—comfort, encouragement, tough love, instruction—I offered it. At the end of that game, I was so exhausted, it was like I'd played all ninety minutes. The starters had left it all on the field; I'd left it all on the bench.

I did that again and again throughout the entire tournament. We won the World Cup that year. We celebrated together—starters and bench players—as one team. I know in my bones that one of the reasons we won the 2015 World Cup was the support of the bench. The pride I feel about how I handled that tournament rivals the pride I have about scoring any big goal.

You'll feel benched sometimes, too. You might not make a team you try out for, or get the lead role in the school play. The stakes might be even higher. You might not get into the high school or college of your choice, or you might be sidelined by the flu on the day of a major exam. Here's what's important: You are allowed to be disappointed when it feels like life's benched you. What you aren't allowed to do is miss your opportunity to lead from whatever bench you're on.

Five days before I was set to travel to the Olympics in China as co-captain of our team, we played an exhibition game and I got the worst injury of my life: two major breaks in my leg that would take many months to heal. I knew immediately I wouldn't be able to travel to the Olympics. My heartbreak rivaled the pain from my broken bones. But I had to do something. So I feverishly typed an email to my teammates, reminding them each of the special talents and fight they brought to the team, and to promise them (and remind myself) that it was okay that they moved on without me. *I can safely say*, I wrote, *that I have no doubt you all will rise to the occasion. No doubt at all, because that's what this team is, has been, and will always be. It's timeless and no one person decides our fate.*

If you're not a leader on the bench, don't call yourself a leader on the field.

You're either a leader everywhere or nowhere.

When I was younger, I was chatting with some friends one day when one of them negatively reacted to a story I told by saying, "That's so gay."

It stung.

Then another friend looked at her and said, "Wait, what do you mean by that?"

The friend who had made the insensitive remark giggled nervously and said, "It was just a joke! I was joking. I was just trying to say it was a silly story!"

As she said that, we all understood—even her—the ridiculousness and cruelty of using the word *gay* to mean bad. It became clear that insults are never a joke. They make room for lies that place marginalized people—people of color, people who are women, people who are disabled, people who are poor, people who are queer—in even more danger. Words matter. Being kind with our words is the same thing as being kind with our world.

Kids who call out bullying or discrimination, kids who sit next to the new kid in the cafeteria, kids who say "I'm sorry" when they hurt someone's feelings—those kids are all brave, they're all leaders.

Every person is the leader of their own life, at any age. Do not give up that power. Claim it. Value it. Use it. Leadership is not just the adult at the head of the table. It's every person—regardless of age—who is allowing their own voice to guide their life. It's every kid speaking up and showing up to build a better world.

So what does it look like for young people to embrace leadership? It looks like volunteering at the local food pantry, speaking encouraging words to a friend, and holding the hand of your little brother when he's scared. It's saying to our families and friends: *No. We don't do unkindness here.* It's running for student-body president and bringing a meal to a sick neighbor. Leadership is taking care of yourself and empowering others to do the same.

Leadership is not a position to earn; it's every single person's right to claim.

Leadership is the blood that runs through your veins—it's born in you.

It's not the privilege of a few; it is the right and responsibility of all.

Leader is not a title that the world gives to you—it's an offering that you give to the world.

CALL TO THE WOLFPACK:

If you have a voice, you have influence to spread.
If you have relationships, you have hearts to guide.
If you know younger people, you have futures to mold.
If you have privilege, you have power to share.
If you have money, you have support to give.
If you know an adult, you have a voter to persuade.
If you have pain, you have empathy to offer.
If you have freedom, you have others to fight for.
If you are alive, you are a leader.

FOUR

MAKE FAILURE YOUR FUEL

Old Rule: Failure means you're out of the game.

New Rule: Failure means you're finally IN the game.

When I was on the youth national team and dreaming of one day playing alongside the legendary soccer star Mia Hamm, I had the opportunity to visit the locker room of the U.S. Women's National Team. Time stopped for me as I looked around and tried to memorize everything I saw: my heroes' grass-stained cleats, their names and numbers hanging above their lockers, their uniforms folded neatly on their chairs.

But the image that stayed with me forever was something else entirely.

What I remember most vividly is a five-by-seven photograph.

Someone had taped this small picture next to the

door so it would be the last thing every player saw before she headed out to the training field.

You might guess that it was a picture of a celebration, the team cheering their last big win or standing on a podium accepting gold medals. But it wasn't. It was a picture of their longtime rival—the Norwegian national team—celebrating after having just beaten the USA in the 1995 World Cup. It was a picture of their own team's last defeat.

Five years later, I was called up to that national team. One day we were on the road with nothing to do but sit around a big table in the dining hall and pass around stories for hours. I mustered up the courage to ask about that picture. I needed to know what it meant to them, so I asked:

"Hey, what was the deal with the picture you kept on the locker room wall of the Norwegian team? Why did you want that to be the last thing you looked at before you went out to play?"

They smiled, and it became clear to me that they'd been waiting for the rookie to start asking the right questions. They began to explain to me that the first order of national-team business is to win. But that when failure does come, the team isn't afraid of it; the team is fueled by it. The team never denies its last failure. We don't reject it. We don't accept it as proof that we aren't worthy of playing at the highest level. Instead, we insist upon remembering. Because we know that the lessons of yesterday's loss become the fuel for tomorrow's win.

I asked, "Do you think putting that picture up worked?"

Our captain at the time, Julie Foudy, said, "Well, we brought home our first Olympic gold the following year. What do you think?"

I left that table understanding that in order to become a champion—on and off the field—I'd need to spend my life transforming my failures into my fuel.

When I was a young player, I had a lot of raw talent, and was starting to accumulate major trophies and awards. One year I was selected to play at a special training camp where we got to scrimmage against professional players. After the game the head coach called me into his office. I figured he wanted to praise me for scoring the most goals. Maybe he wanted to move me up to a higher level.

Instead, he said that I just wasn't good enough yet.

He listed specifics where I had fallen short. And he said that since I wasn't trying hard enough to improve my game, my teammates couldn't count on me. He wasn't going to take the risk. He cut me from the next camp.

I fumed silently as I walked out the door. *How could he?* I felt defensive and devastated, like I'd been punched in the gut. His criticism knocked the wind out of me. But as I let his words roll around in my head for the next month I realized he was right.

This was the first time in my life I had truly failed at soccer—and I had a decision to make. I had to decide whether I would accept what the coach said to me as the end or the beginning. As a rejection or a challenge. I decided to make myself vulnerable. To try again and try harder. So I wrote him an email saying that I understood his criticism, and would work harder than ever on the things he told me to work on. At the end of the email, I asked him to give me another chance.

He responded immediately: "That's exactly what I wanted to hear."

When we feel powerless in the face of failure, it's hard to remember that failure offers us a choice. We still have so much power, because we decide what we do next.

Will you disappoint your parents? Will you underperform in school? Will you be left off the roster, lose the class election, fall short of a goal you set for yourself? Of course you will! Everyone fails. But only the wise know how to turn failure into their fuel.

When you fail, you have three choices: Blame, Shame, or Claim.

Blame: We can blame someone else for our mistake.

I used to do this all the time on the field when I was young. If I missed an important shot, I gestured toward a teammate, suggesting that it was her fault because she'd made a bad pass. I was hoping that if I blamed somebody else, the people on the sidelines wouldn't blame me.

Shame: We can crumble and quit after our mistake.

I had a friend who used to let a single mistake on the field take her out of the entire game. Each time she missed a shot she'd crumble in a heap, give up— making the rest of the game harder for all of us.

There is a third choice we can make after a failure: Claim.

I had another teammate who did two important

things every time she made a mistake. She yelled *My bad* and then, immediately following the mistake—she took her play to another level. Every single time she lost the ball, instead of wasting the next moment on blame or shame, she did everything in her power to get that ball back. She turned the embarrassment of failure into fuel to fix her mistake. She *claimed*.

Do you know people like this? People who point and blame after their mistakes? People who crumble in shame after their mistakes? People who claim and fix their mistakes?

Let's stop worrying, *What if I fail?* Instead, let's commit to this: *WHEN I fail, I'll claim it, fix it, and keep trying.*

The world needs to see young people take risks, fail big, and insist on their right to stick around and try again. And again. And again. A champion never allows a short-term failure to take them out of the long-term game. If you don't give up, you can never lose.

CALL TO THE WOLFPACK:

Try. Fail.

Claim it.

Then transform Failure into your Fuel.

FIVE

CHAMPION EACH OTHER

Old Rule: Be against each other.
New Rule: Be FOR each other.

During every ninety-minute soccer game there are a few magical moments when the ball actually hits the back of the net and a goal is scored. When this happens, it means that everything has come together perfectly—the perfect pass, the perfectly timed run, every player in the precise place at exactly the right time—culminating in a moment in which one player scores that goal.

What happens next on that team is what transforms a group of individual people into one team. The bench erupts. Teammates from all over the field rush toward the goal scorer. There are high fives, chest bumps, dances, hugs, and a spontaneous celebratory huddle that disperses as quickly as it began.

It might appear to the crowd that the team is

celebrating the goal scorer, but what the team is really celebrating is every player, every coach, every practice, every sprint, every doubt, and every failure that this one single goal represents.

Sometimes you will make a sixty-yard sprint only to watch another player score the big goal. Sometimes it was your tackle, your run, your heart, and your sweat that made that goal possible.

You will not always be the goal scorer. When you are not, you better be rushing toward them.

Sometimes you will be the goal scorer.

I was that goal scorer 184 times during my international career.

If you watch videos of any of those goals, you'll see that the moment after I score, I begin to point.

I point to the teammate who assisted.

I point to the defender who protected us.

I point to the midfielder who ran tirelessly.

I point to the coach who dreamed up this play.

I point to the bench player who willed this moment into existence.

I've never scored a goal in my life without getting a pass from someone else.

Every goal I ever scored belonged to my entire team.

When you score, start pointing.
When someone else scores, start rushing.

We can point and rush off the field, too. Though I don't play soccer anymore, I still love to celebrate successes with my new team: my family. We continue a tradition that my former captain, Julie Foudy, started with her family. The "High-Low-Cheer." We go around the dinner table and each one of us downloads about our day. First, a nod to the best thing that happened to them that day (high); then the worst thing that they encountered (low); and finally a shout-out about something terrific someone else did (cheer). It's a great way to reflect on the good, practice confronting the bad, and get into the mindset of seeing the light of others.

Let's all start talking openly about our successes and mistakes with the people we love. Let's help each other.

Let's rush toward each other. Let's stop believing that joy, success, and attention are like pies that must be divvied up—so more for them means less for me. We will remember that these things are infinite, so there is more than enough to go around.

CALL TO THE WOLFPACK:

Their victory is your victory. Celebrate with them.
Your victory is their victory. Point to them.

SIX

DEMAND THE BALL

Old Rule: Play it safe. Pass the ball.
New Rule: Believe in yourself. Demand the ball.

When I was a younger player, my heroes were the women of the national team. Among them was Michelle Akers, the best player in the world. Michelle was tall like I am, built like I'd be built, and the most courageous soccer player I'd ever seen play. She lived out every one of my dreams.

Since there was no professional women's league at the time, Michelle had to find different ways to train between national team games. So, one day, our youth national team found ourselves preparing to play alongside our hero. We were eighteen years old and there was Michelle Akers—a chiseled powerhouse of a woman, a world champion, a legend. Our hands shook as we laced up our cleats. We were playing a scrimmage— five against five. For the first three quarters of play,

Michelle was taking it easy on us, coaching us, teaching us about spacing, timing, and the tactics of the game. At the start of the fourth quarter, Michelle realized that because of all of this coaching, her team was losing by three goals. In that moment, we saw a light switch on inside of her.

She ran back to her own goalkeeper, stood one yard away from her, and screamed:

GIVE. ME. THE. BALL.

The goalkeeper gave her the ball.

And Michelle took that ball and dribbled through our entire team and she scored.

This game was "winners keepers," meaning that if you scored, you got the ball back. So after Michelle scored, the ball went right back to her goalkeeper.

And so did Michelle. She ran back to her goalie, and again stood a yard away from her and screamed:

GIVE ME THE BALL.

The keeper gave her the ball.

And again Michelle dribbled through us and scored.

And then she did it again. And again. Until she'd taken her team to victory.

What I saw in Michelle that day changed how I saw myself forever.

Before that game, I had always tried to turn down my talent and dim my light to avoid outshining others. I thought it was the humble thing to do. I was afraid that my talent would intimidate others and might drive a wedge between my teammates and me. So on the field, I operated at 75 percent.

But watching Michelle, I saw the power of one woman's competitive fire. I saw a woman who not only wanted to win, but owned that desire, and believed that she could be the one to make it happen.

That game marked the moment I stopped pretending to be less powerful than I know I am.

The most inspiring thing on earth is believing in yourself, giving 100 percent, and owning your greatness unapologetically.

Watching Michelle use her power shamelessly freed me to use mine, too.

I think about Michelle every time I'm tempted to decide I'm unworthy, unprepared, incapable, or not good enough.

Four years ago, I fell in love with a woman who has three children: Chase, Tish, and Amma. I'd always wanted to be a mother, but I felt completely unprepared to be a stepparent. I kept coming back to the horror stories I'd heard about stepmothers and their children. I felt afraid that the kids would resent me and would never see me as their true parent. I worried I'd be incapable of earning their love and respect, arriving this far down the road of their lives. Would I be good enough? I didn't know.

But I decided that when you want something as badly as I wanted a life with Glennon—when you want something as badly as I wanted a family—you just have to show up before you're ready and demand the ball.

That didn't mean, though, that I could just throw myself into the kids' lives. In this case, it was the kids who demanded the ball. I may have been the adult, but it was up to them to decide when they would open their hearts to me. It was hard and I had to be very patient. Eventually, they began to invite me into their Pack. By the end of the following year, I was coaching Tish and Amma's soccer team and all three kids were calling me their "bonus mom."

If one of your friends is going through a big change in their family, grab the ball and check in on them—they may need a little extra support, even if they don't ask for it. And if you are going through a transition like this in your family, I hope you can remember that it's new turf for everyone—for the kids and for the parents—and everyone is figuring it out as they go along. We're all just showing up, ready to play.

Becoming Glennon's wife and my children's bonus mom was the best decision I've ever made in my life. Is it easy? Heck no. Every day I have moments filled with doubt about my parenting decisions. But Glennon, the kids' dad, Craig, the kids, and I are a Pack. We threw away the old stories about blended families and decided to write a new one. Our themes are respect, grace, and the constant decision to value collective peace over our individual egos.

Sometimes I look at my family and think: *What if I'd decided not to become a mother until I felt ready, or until I'd secured certainty that I'd never make a mistake?* I'd have missed the best thing that's ever happened to me. I also would have missed my opportunity to help other families like mine. Every day I hear from people who are using our family as inspiration to write their own unique and beautiful stories about blended families.

In the end, owning and unleashing all your power isn't just about you. It's also about the domino effect. When you stand up and demand the ball, you give others permission to do the same. The Wolfpack's collective power begins by unleashing the power of each individual Wolf.

As Rudyard Kipling wrote in *The Second Jungle Book*:

The strength of the Pack is the Wolf, and the strength of the Wolf is the Pack.

CALL TO THE WOLFPACK:

Believe in yourselves. Stand up and say:
GIVE ME THE BALL.
GIVE ME THE OPPORTUNITY. GIVE ME THE
MICROPHONE. GIVE ME THE POWER.
GIVE ME THE RESPECT I DESERVE—AND
GIVE IT TO MY WOLFPACK, TOO.

SEVEN

BRING IT ALL

Old Rule: Lead with dominance. Create Followers.
New Rule: Lead with your full self. Cultivate Leaders.

When Pia Sundhage was hired as our new coach for the national team, we were the biggest, fittest, strongest, most physically dominant team in the world. We were winning by the sheer force of power and intimidation alone. That was fine with us. The score at the end of the game was the only thing that mattered, period.

The first time Pia met with us, she said:

You are the best in the world. But there is still a higher level in you. You have proven you can win games. What I want you to work on is how you win games. I want us to continue to win, but I want us to win while honoring ourselves, our teammates, our opponents, and the game. We will win

*with creativity, innovation, and steady assuredness
instead of just physical dominance. We will win
beautifully.*

Then she pulled out a guitar and began to sing
"The Times They Are A-Changin'" by Bob Dylan.
Our team sat there, stunned. We stared at this Swedish
woman thinking: *She has absolutely no idea what she's
doing. We're screwed.*

This was the first time many of us had ever seen a
leader make herself vulnerable. We didn't even know
that was allowed—it felt, at first, like a leadership failure. And yet, as we listened to her sing, though we
felt a little awkward, we became curious. Soon, we felt
moved. We felt a part of ourselves awaken. We felt
connected.

Pia brought music to us because Pia loves music. By
showing us who she was and what she loved, she taught
us that real leaders know who they are and bring every
bit of themselves to whomever they lead. Real leaders don't mimic how other leaders look, sound, and
act. They understand that there are as many authentic
ways to lead as there are people.

Looking back, I can see that Pia's impromptu

musical performance was the spark our team needed to begin reimagining our ideas about how to lead, and about who gets to lead.

Before Pia, we subscribed to the old, top-down structure of leadership. Wisdom, direction, and ideas were determined and announced by the coaches and captains, and immediately, without questions or input, executed by the team. Before Pia, our team was made up of a few leaders and dozens of followers. After Pia, our leadership structure was slowly broken down and re-created. Off the field, my role as co-captain became less about making pronouncements to everyone and more about encouraging everyone to share their ideas. Players began to feel safe and brave enough to bring their voices and ideas to the table. On the field, we started coaching each other. The new kid, Alex Morgan, started giving me pointers. Veterans began to learn from newbies; starters began to learn from bench players. Captains began to learn from the strength-and-conditioning coaches. Every single person—from players to support staff—began to think of themselves as a leader.

This new way wasn't always comfortable. It required the new players to be brave, and the veterans like me—who were used to telling, not listening—to instead be humble. But we had Pia as a model. This new way wasn't just a theory to us. If Pia had just told us to be brave, humble, and vulnerable, we would never have been able to embody it. As our leader, she had to show us.

But you don't have to be a coach or a teacher or a parent or hold any formal title to cultivate other leaders. You can be an older sibling or cousin or friend.

I'm the youngest of seven kids and was used to my older brothers and sisters teasing me or dismissing me. The summer when I was fourteen, I really wanted to go to my beloved summer camp, which I had attended every summer since I could remember. But I had also started to play soccer at a high level, so my mom insisted that I go to soccer camp. We were at a stand-off, and as I stormed upstairs to my room I announced to my older brother that I was quitting soccer.

He stopped dead in his tracks and looked me in the eye. "You are so gifted," he said, and he begged me not to give it up. "I would give anything to have half your talent."

I was shocked, and so moved. It probably wasn't easy for him to let his annoying little sister know she was better at something than he was. But it was his vulnerability that convinced me to stay in the game. I wanted to honor the faith that he and my other brothers and sisters had in me.

The old way is to lead with invulnerability and collect followers.

The new way is to lead with your whole self—and inspire a team of leaders.

CALL TO THE WOLFPACK:

Claim your power, and bring along your full self.
Clear the way for others to do the same.
Because what our families,
our communities,
and the world needs
is nothing more—and nothing less—
than exactly who we are.

EIGHT

FIND YOUR PACK

Old Rule: You're on your own.
**New Rule: You're not alone. You've got your
Pack.**

Recently, I decided to join my friend Mel in a running challenge. We committed to running on our own every day and sending each other our distances for accountability. After thirty years of training, I figured that this challenge would be a piece of cake.

The challenge was not a piece of cake. It was miserable. I hated every single minute of every single run. It was like I had lead in my feet, like I'd never run before. My survival mantra as I gasped for air was: *This hurts. This hurts. Don't stop. Don't stop.*

One night, I said to Glennon, "Listen, I've never liked running, but I've also never hated it this much.

Why does it feel so impossible all of a sudden? I was a professional athlete! I used to train six hours a day! Could I have lost all of my athleticism in the last three years?"

She said, "Babe, you haven't lost your athleticism. The difference is that you don't have your teammates running with you anymore. You used to run with your Pack. Now you're a lone wolf out there."

She was right. My entire life I'd been surrounded by teammates suffering with me, encouraging me, making me laugh, and distracting me from my worries. Our pain was lessened because we shared it. Life is harder as a lone wolf. We all need a Pack.

When Barnard posted my Wolfpack speech online, it went viral.

People I've admired my whole life—world leaders, celebrities, athletes, and activists—shared my words with their communities. People circulated it to their companies, schools, friend groups, and classrooms. Parents turned my speech into art and hung paintings of wolves on their children's bedroom walls. One mom even told me that it had become her daughters' new bedtime story.

What impacted me most was not how wide the message went—but how deep it went.

I've saved notes like this one, from a 12-year-old named Jaye, to read when I'm tempted to forget that showing up matters.

Thank you for the bravery you showed in your speech. You reminded me of the wolf inside me. People are always making me feel like I can't make a difference, because I'm a kid. But I know that's not true. I know if I listen to my wolf and find my pack, I can make a difference in this world.

Whether you're a soccer player, math whiz, poet, ballet dancer, debater—whoever you are—you need a brave and honest crew to support you. You need them to hold you accountable to your greatness, remind you of who you are, and join you to change the world.

You need a Pack.

The question is: How do you build one?

In a way, I had it easy. I played a team sport so I always had a ready-made group of girls and women who became my Pack. That's not going to be the case for everyone.

Maybe it isn't easy for you to make friends in your middle school. That's a signal to be on the lookout for activities you enjoy where you'll eventually find others who share your passions. Maybe you're new to the neighborhood and haven't gotten adjusted yet. That's okay—in time you'll find your place. Maybe you're super popular and have friends in every group. That's an opportunity to welcome the newer kids, or the kids who have a harder time fitting in. Maybe you have a vibrant and wild imagination that keeps you company. Write down or paint or perform your stories! You never know who else might be inspired by them.

I know from my own life that when you're inexperienced at anything—when you don't know what to do or how to begin—all you can do is show up, awkwardly and nervously sometimes, and try.

So I'm going to try. I'm going to gather the people I respect, admire, and trust most. I'm going to support them when they need it and ask them for help when I need it.

You can, too. You can change our lives and our world by knowing the power of your Wolf and the strength of your Pack.

CALL TO THE WOLFPACK:

Life is not meant to be lived as a Lone Wolf.
We all need a Pack.

TIME TO CHANGE THE GAME

On the night of my final game, after seventeen years as a collegiate, professional, and national team player, I decided to release a farewell message to the sport to which I had given so much of my life— and to the players, teams, and fans who had given so much of their lives to me.

My final message to the game: *Forget Me*.

In it, I sat on a metal chair cleaning out my locker, pondering the legacy I'd leave. The screen flashed with images of little girls scoring goals, young women running sprints, and a teenage boy wearing my jersey.

While the clips rolled, I said this:

Forget me. Forget my number. Forget my name. Forget I ever existed.

Forget the medals won, the records broken, and the sacrifices made.

I want to leave a legacy where the ball keeps rolling forward. Where the next generation accomplishes things so great that I am no longer remembered.

So—Forget me. Because the day I'm forgotten is the day we will succeed.

Since 2013 I held the world record for most goals scored—by any man or woman. I've been grateful-to-the-bones for the path the Pack before me tread so that I could spend my life playing the game I love.

And now as I write this book I am celebrating the honor of passing that record to the great Christine Sinclair: the new world-record holder for most international goals—by any man or woman—in history.

On the day we learned the news about Christine's record-breaking goal, Tish joked, "Oh great, now what do I say? My mom's number two?"

It was funny. But I'd be lying if I didn't admit to a moment of sadness and fear when I passed that record on. Who was I now if not the number one goal scorer of all time?

But then Amma said, "Yeah, but Abby's the number one bonus mom in the world. No one can take that from her."

Even though a part of me was sad when Christine broke my record, I made a decision. I would embody everything I claimed to believe. I would champion Christine. I would rush toward her. I would remember and remind everyone else that Christine's victory is the victory of the entire Pack.

My dream has always been to leave a legacy ensuring the future success of the sport I'd dedicated my life to. I wanted little girls coming up after me to accomplish things I'd only dreamed of.

A few years ago I started coaching Tish's soccer team. As a matter of fact, I coached them all the way to the championship. I didn't talk about my career much because I was committed to keeping the focus on them—but I secretly enjoyed that these kids knew an Olympian was leading them.

Then one day, near the end of our season, when I

was warming the team up and telling a story about my retirement, one of my players looked up at me and said, "So what did you retire from?"

I paused for a moment, wondering if she was joking. She wasn't.

I looked down at her and I said, "Um. SOCCER."

And she said, "Oh. Who did you play for?"

I widened my eyes and said, "THE. UNITED. STATES. OF. AMERICA."

And she said, "Huh. Cool. Wait . . . does that mean you know Alex Morgan?!!"

Be careful what you wish for. They forgot me.

Seriously, though, others not knowing who I was didn't bother me.

What scared me was that without soccer, *I* didn't know who I was.

When I took off my jersey for the last time, I lost the identity that I'd proudly worn since I was five years old: Abby Wambach, soccer player.

Without soccer, who was I?

One night I told Glennon how afraid I was that when I lost soccer, I'd lost myself. The next day, she wrote me this:

Abby,

What is most special about you isn't your talent on the soccer field.

When people look at you, they notice something about you that's different.

It's the way you carry yourself and the way you treat people. It's about your dignity mixed with your ferocity. It's about your particular beauty that stands in stark contrast to the manufactured beauty that women have been sold. It's about how you stand and run and talk.

It's a little bit about your hair.

You are a walking glorious rebellion. What you release into the world rekindles a fire inside of us that the world put out long ago.

I don't think the magic was on the field, Abby. I think the magic is inside of you. I think you'll carry it with you till you die. From out here, Abby, it is crystal clear that soccer didn't make you special—you made soccer special. You have lost nothing. You take it all with you. Soccer led us to you. Now we'll follow. Not because of you as an athlete, because of you, my Abby.

She was right. You know who I am now? I'm still the same Abby. I still show up and give 100 percent—now to my new Pack—and I still fight every day to make a better future for the next generation.

You see, soccer didn't make me who I am. I brought who I am to soccer, and I get to bring who I am wherever I go.

So do you.

Right now, I bet a lot is changing for you. You're probably spending more time with friends or doing activities away from home, turning toward the wider world, a world that is both exciting and uncertain. That can be scary and confusing and frustrating. It can also be beautiful and thrilling and magical. A moment of change is also a moment of choice. In your new world, you get to choose who you want to be.

So as you head into your future, think about your choices. But don't just ask yourself, "What do I want to do?" Ask yourself, "Who do I want to be?"

The most important thing I've learned is that what you do will never define you for long. Who you are always will.

You are the Wolves.

There is magic inside of you. There is power among you.

Storm the valleys together and change the world forever.

NEW RULES

1. Create your own path.

2. Be grateful for what you have AND demand what you deserve.

3. Lead now—from wherever you are.

4. Failure means you're finally IN the game.

5. Be FOR each other.

6. Believe in yourself. Demand the ball.

7. Lead with your full self. Cultivate Leaders.

8. You're not alone. You've got your Pack.

ACKNOWLEDGMENTS

Thank you to Margaret Riley King, my agent and friend.

Thank you to Kate Meltzer, my editor and pack mate.

Thank you to Ruby Shamir, whose collaboration and creativity helped bring this book to life.

Thank you to Glennon, Chase, Tish, and Amma, who bring me to life.

ABOUT THE AUTHOR

Abby Wambach is a two-time Olympic gold medalist, FIFA World Cup champion, and six-time winner of the U.S. Soccer Athlete of the Year award. She is an activist for equality and inclusion, and the #1 *New York Times* bestselling author of *Wolfpack* and *Forward: A Memoir*. Abby co-founded Wolfpack Endeavor, which is revolutionizing leadership development for women in the workplace and beyond. She lives in Florida with her wife and three children.